ORIGAMI

The Japanese Art of
Paper Folding

ORIGAMI – THE JAPANESE ART OF PAPER FOLDING

Published by Tuttle Publishing, an imprint of Periplus Editions (HK) Ltd.,
with editorial offices at 153 Milk Street, Boston, Massachusetts 02109

Published as part of Deluxe Origami
Not to be sold separately

ISBN: 0-8048-3085-1

Distributed by

North America, Latin America and Europe
Tuttle Publishing
364 Innovation Drive
North Clarendon, VT 05759-9436
Tel: (802) 773 8930
Fax: (802) 773 6993
Email: info@tuttlepublishing.com
www.tuttlepublishing.com

Japan
Tuttle Publishing
Yaekari Building, 3rd Floor
5-4-12 Ōsaki, Shinagawa-ku
Tokyo 141-0032
Tel: (03) 5437 0171
Fax: (03) 5437 0755
Email: tuttle-sales@gol.com

Asia Pacific
Berkeley Books Pte. Ltd.
130 Joo Seng Road, #06-01/03
Singapore 368357
Tel: (65) 6280 1330
Fax: (65) 6280 6290
Email: inquiries@periplus.com.sg
www.periplus.com

10 09 08 07 06 05 04
9 8 7 6 5 4 3

Printed in Hong Kong

Contents

Introduction

Origami, the stimulating hobby of paper-folding, is a favorite pastime with the Japanese, especially children. Some of the extremely complicated designs that can be created with only a piece of paper and some nimble fingers are truly astonishing. For the beginner, simpler designs are provided along with those which, with practice and patience, can be learned by anyone who would like to master an art that has flourished in Japan for more than ten centuries.

The most difficult object in this book to make is the crane, but then, it is also the most fun, and once you have mastered it, it will be a real achievement. In Japan, the crane is a symbol of good luck and can be found, in some form or other, practically any place—even in some of the designs on women's kimonos. Often, folded cranes of all sizes are strung on pieces of thread and hung from the ceiling to decorate a room. They also have a religious meaning, especially in rural areas, where they are hung from the ceilings of shrines and temples as offerings from the people who go there to pray.

Generally, colored paper about four to seven inches square is used. For a mixed-color effect, two sheets of different colors may be used by placing them back to back. For the present, however, I suggest that the following points be kept in mind:

1. All of the objects illustrated in the diagrams of this book are to be made from squarepieces of paper. Five- or seven-inch squares are the easiest to work with. Use the paper provided or any thin paper, not heavy construction or art paper.

2. It is a good idea to practice making an object with ordinary paper so as not to waste colored paper.

3. If the directions seem to be complicated, you can mark the corners of the paper to correspond with the markings in the diagrams. The instructions can be more easily followed in this way.

4. Begin folding with the white side of the paper up, unless the instructions say to begin with the colored side.

5. Always make sharp creases. It helps to use your fingernail, an ice cream stick, or a rule.

6. When following each step-by-step instruction, it helps to look at the next drawing. This will show you how the folded piece should look.

Dolls

1. Fold a square piece of paper (Fig. 1) so that the edge of AB extends over as far as the center line AC as shown in Fig. 2.

2. Do the same with AD in order to get Fig. 3.

3. Fold along MN so that point C is over and above points B and D. See Fig. 4.

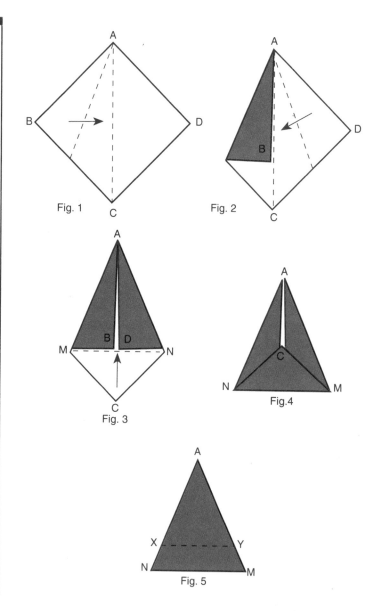

Fig. 1

Fig. 2

Fig. 3

Fig.4

Fig. 5

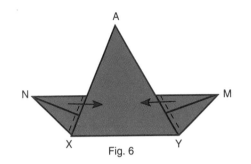

A

N   M

X   Y

Fig. 6

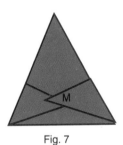

M

Fig. 7

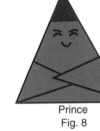

Prince
Fig. 8

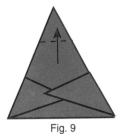

Fig. 9

Princess
Fig. 10

4. Turn the paper over and fold back MN along XY about one-third of the way up (Fig. 5) to get Fig.6.

5. Fold points M and N forward along AY and AX so as to overlap each other as in Fig. 7.

6. Complete the doll by drawing the face (Fig. 8).

7. To make a princess (Fig. 10), fold back the top of the head as shown in Fig. 9.

Clown

1. Fold a square piece of paper along lines DE and DF (Fig. 1) so that edges BD and CD meet at the center AD (Fig. 2).

2. Cut MN and PO approximately 3/4 of the way to the center (Fig. 2).

3. Fold along AN and AO (Fig. 3) so that the two side flaps overlap each other (Fig. 4).

4. Cut slit XY about the length of NO and slightly less than half an inch below EF (Fig. 4).

5. Fold along EF (Fig. 4), bring point A forward and through slit XY (Fig. 5).

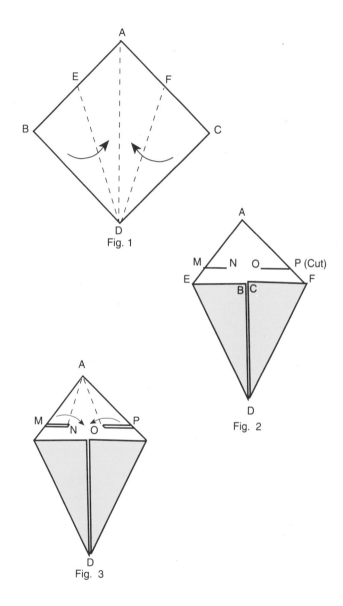

Fig. 1

Fig. 2

Fig. 3

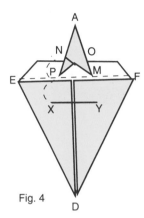

Fig. 4

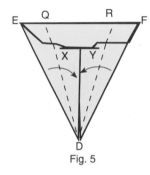

Fig. 5

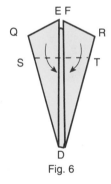

Fig. 6

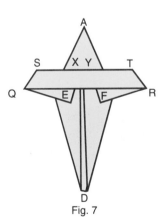

Fig. 7

6. Fold along QD and RD (Fig. 5) so that points E and F meet at the center (Fig. 6).

7. Fold along ST (Fig. 6), bringing QR forward, and point A will come up by itself (Fig. 7). Line ST is on XY.

8. To make the legs, cut the lower part of AD from D (Fig. 7).

9. Turn the paper over and draw the face.

9

Crane

1. Fold a square piece of paper at line BC so that point A is over point D (Figs. 1 & 2).

2. Fold at ED so that point B is over point C (Fig. 3).

3. As shown in Figs. 3 and 4, open B and bring it over until it is directly above D. Crease paper along EF and EG.

4. Turn it over and you will have Fig. 5. Do the same with C as you did with B and the result is Fig. 6.

5. Crease at YC and ZC (Fig. 7) so that points H and I meet along line EC, and then unfold.

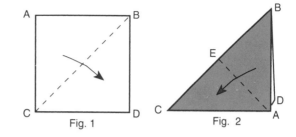

Fig. 1

Fig. 2

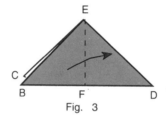

Fig. 3

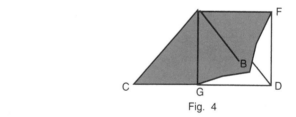

Fig. 4

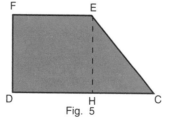

Fig. 5

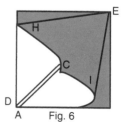

Fig. 6

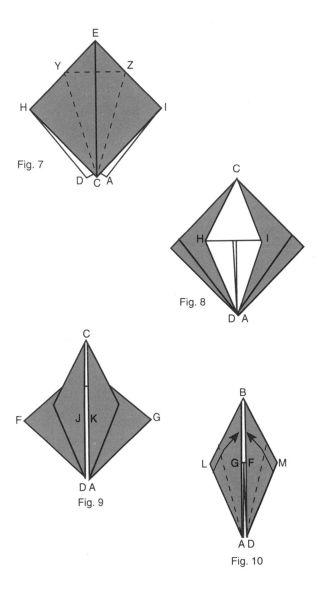

Fig. 7

Fig. 8

Fig. 9

Fig. 10

6. Lift up C and fold at YZ so that H and I meet at the middle along line AC. Fig. 8 shows this step being executed and Fig. 9 shows the completion.

7. Turn the paper over and repeat steps 5 and 6. Resulting in Fig. 10.

8. Fold on the dotted line shown in Fig. 10 so that L and M meet at the middle along lines BA and BD (Fig. 11).

9. Turn the paper over and fold J and K the same way you did L and M. The result is shown in Fig. 12.

10. Lift A up toward the right as shown in Fig. 13 and fold at K. In doing so reverse the fold down the middle of this flap, forming the neck.

11. Next make the head and then fold D to the left to make the tail. Head, neck, and tail are made in the same way as those of the swan.

12. To complete, spread the wings (C and B) open and blow through the hole indicated in Fig. 14 in order to swell out the body.

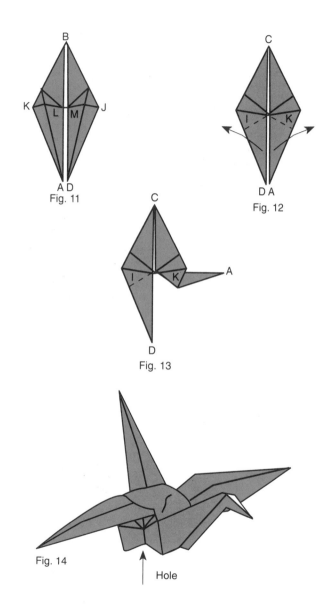

Fig. 11

Fig. 12

Fig. 13

Fig. 14

Hole

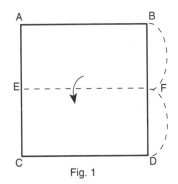

Fig. 1

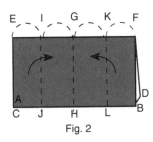

Fig. 2

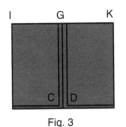

Fig. 3

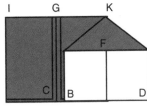

Fig. 4

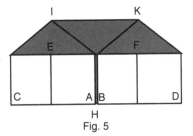

Fig. 5

House

1. Fold a square piece of paper at EF (Fig. 1) so that edge AB is on top of edge CD as in Fig. 2.

2. Fold the edges AEC and BFD forward so that they meet at the center line GH as shown in Fig. 3.

3. Separate points B and D by holding B in place and swinging point D over to the right, thus bringing point F to the position shown in Fig.4.

4. Do the same with points ECA (swinging C to the left) and you will have the paper house shown in Fig. 5.

Candy Box

1. Fold a square piece of paper along line BD (Fig.1) so that corner A falls on corner C (Fig. 2).

2. Fold along EA (Fig 2) so that corner D falls on B (Fig. 3).

3. Open corner D (Fig. 3) and bring it over to the right until it is directly above A (Fig. 4). Then crease along EF and EG (Fig. 5).

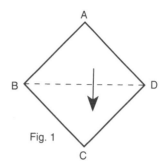

Fig. 1

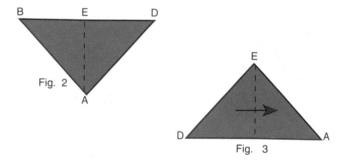

Fig. 2

Fig. 3

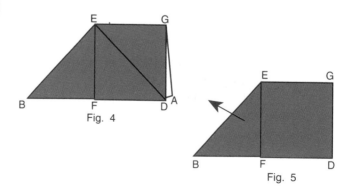

Fig. 4

Fig. 5

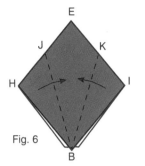

Fig. 6

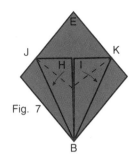

Fig. 7

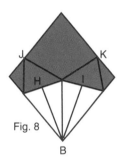

Fig. 8

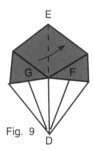

Fig. 9

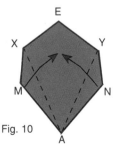

Fig. 10

4. Turn the paper over and repeat step 3 with B as in Fig. 6.

5. Fold along BJ and BK (Fig. 6) so that BH and BI meet at BE (Fig. 7).

6. Open the corners H and I (Fig. 7) so that JH falls on JB and KI falls on KB (Fig. 8).

7. Turn the paper over and repeat steps 5 and 6 (Fig. 9).

8. Fold only the top flap along ED (Fig. 9), and bring G on top of F. Then turn the paper over and bring I on top of H (Fig. 10).

9. Fold along XA and YA (Fig. 10) so that MA and NA meet at EA (Fig. 11).

10. Fold along QR (Fig. 11), bringing point A forward and up (Fig. 12).

11. Fold along OP (Figs. 12 and 13).

12. Turn the paper over and repeat steps 9, 10, and 11 on the other side with corner C, and then with B and D (Fig. 14).

13. Carefully insert your fingers into the candy box and flatten E (Fig. 15).

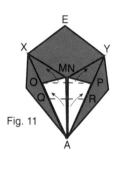

Fig. 11

Fig. 12

Fig. 13

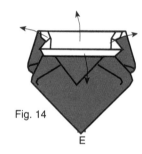

Fig. 14

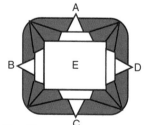

Fig. 15

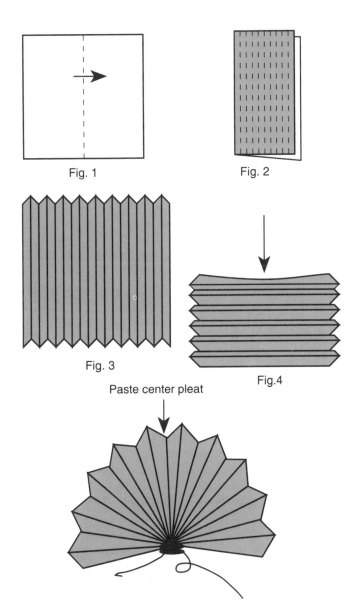

Fig. 1

Fig. 2

Fig. 3

Fig.4

Paste center pleat

Fan

1. Take a square piece of paper and fold in half (Fig. 1). Make lengthwise folds (accordion fashion) across the entire breadth of the paper (Fig. 2) and then open to get Fig. 3.

2. Fold in half as shown in Fig. 4 then paste the center pleats together.

3. To complete, tie a piece of string about one-half inch up from the bottom. See Fig. 5.

Pinwheel

1. Take a square sheet of paper and fold it so that AC and BD (Fig. 1) meet at the center line EF and look like Fig. 2.

2. Fold OM back along the line QR so that OM meets PN. This will result in Fig. 3.

3. Fold along ST so that PN meets QR as in Fig. 4. Note that flap OM remains where it is for the present.

4. Pull out corners D and C as in Fig. 5.

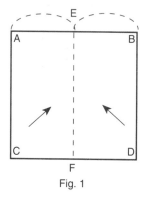

Fig. 1

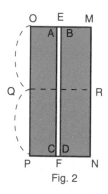

Fig. 2

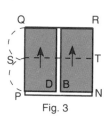

Fig. 3

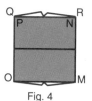

Fig. 4

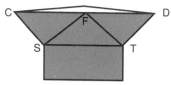

Fig. 5

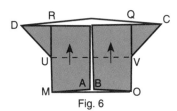

Fig. 6

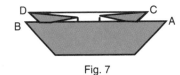

Fig. 7

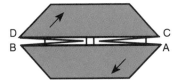

Fig. 8

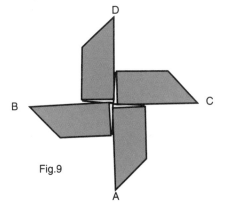

Fig.9

5. Turn the paper over and fold so that MO meets RQ (Fig. 6). Pull out corners A and B and you will get Fig. 7.

6. Spread out Fig. 7 resulting in Fig. 8.

7. Fold corner D upward and corner A downward and you will get Fig. 9.

Flowers

1. Fold a square sheet of paper down the middle (Fig. 1) at EF in order to get Fig. 2.

2. Crease in the middle at GH and reopen.

3. Bring the corner F up between D and B so that it meets G, thus placing HF along GH. See Fig. 3. DHB will then form an upside-down triangle.

4. Repeat the step with E (Fig. 4).

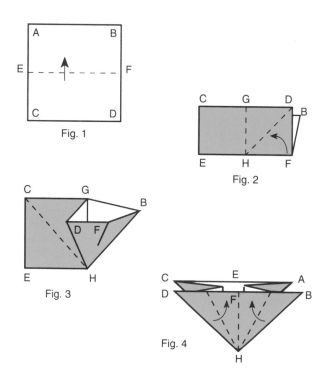

Fig. 1

Fig. 2

Fig. 3

Fig. 4

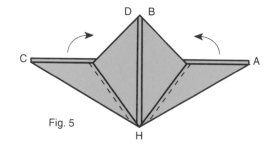

Fig. 5

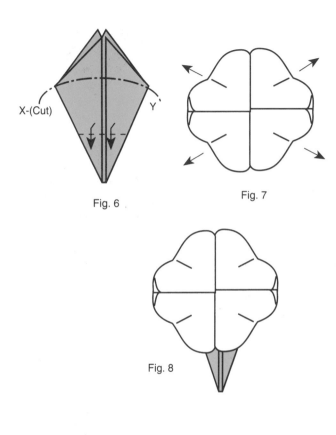

X-(Cut)　　　　　Y

Fig. 6

Fig. 7

Fig. 8

Fig. 9

5. Bring the corners B and D forward to meet at the center over FH as in Fig. 5.

6. Turn the paper over and do the same with corners A and C.

7. Cut off the points with a pair of scissors (Fig. 6).

8. Open the petals, as shown in Fig. 7, as far down as XY and you will get Fig. 8.

9. It is possible to make many kinds of flowers by cutting the petals into various shapes. See Fig. 9.

21

Helmet

1. Fold a square piece of paper along line BD (Fig. 1) so that corner A is over corner C as shown in Fig. 2.

2. Fold along EF and EG so that corners B and D meet at point A (Fig. 3).

3. Fold up points B and D so that they meet at E as shown in Fig. 4.

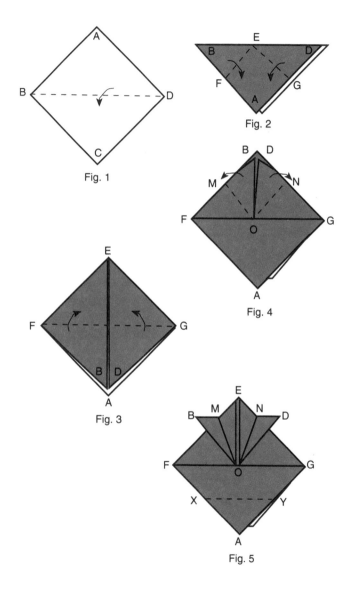

Fig. 1

Fig. 2

Fig. 4

Fig. 3

Fig. 5

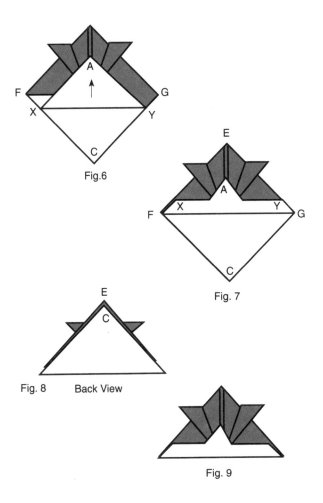

Fig.6

Fig. 7

Fig. 8   Back View

Fig. 9

4. Bring forward point B and fold this flap along OM (Fig. 5). Point M is about one-third of the way down EF.

5. Do the same with point D, folding along ON.

6. Fold at XY (Fig. 6) so that point A is over and above point O.

7. Fold this front flap again at FG to make Fig. 7.

8. Turn over and fold C so it meets E (Fig. 8).

9. Turn over again and the result is Fig. 9.

23

Jet Plane

1. Fold a square piece of paper along EF (Fig. 1) so that corner B meets center O (Fig. 2).

2. Fold along GH (Fig. 2) so that corner C meets B at center O (Fig. 3).

3. Fold along IJ (Fig. 3) so that edge FD meets CH (Fig. 4).

4. Fold along KI (Fig. 4) so that edge AE meets GC (Fig. 5).

5. Fold along line LNM (Fig. 5) so that D falls on F (Fig. 6).

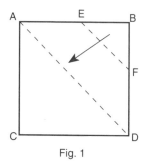

Fig. 1

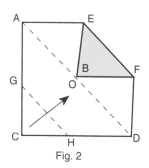

Fig. 2

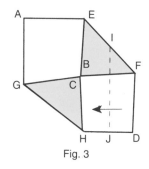

Fig. 3

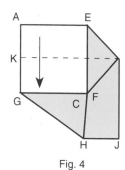

Fig. 4

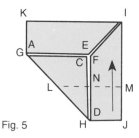

Fig. 5

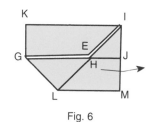

Fig. 6

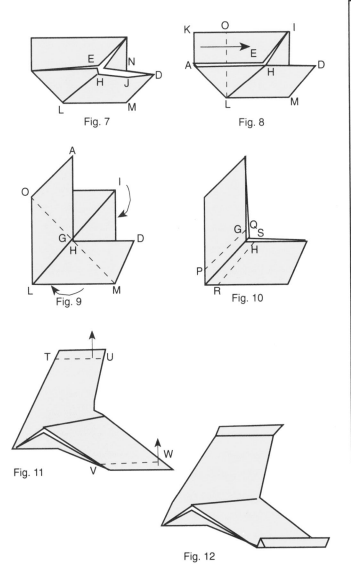

Fig. 7

Fig. 8

Fig. 9

Fig. 10

Fig. 11

Fig. 12

6. Open corner J, bringing corner D to the right, thus making MJ fall on MN (Fig. 7).

7. Repeat steps 5 and 6 with A (Figs. 8 and 9).

8. Fold back I along OM so that corner I falls underneath L (Fig. 9).

9. Fold along PQ and RS so that the two sides touch each other (Fig. 10).

10. Fold along TU and VW (Fig. 11) so that the two edges turn up (Figs. 11 and 12).

25

Kimono

1. Fold a square sheet of paper along line EF (Fig. 1) so AC falls on BD (Fig. 2).

2. Fold forward at GH, about one-quarter of an inch down from EA, and once more at IJ (Figs. 2 and 3).

3. Fold back corners I and J along OM and ON (Fig. 3) so that OI and OJ meet at the center in the back (Fig.4). Point O is halfway between I and J.

4. Fold back point O along PQ and then fold forward along RS so that PQ falls on FC as shown in Figs. 4 and 5.

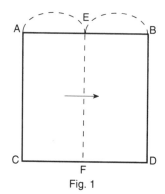

Fig. 1

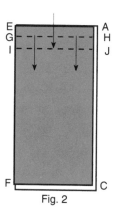

Fig. 2

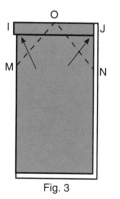

Fig. 3

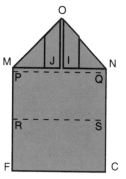

Fig. 4

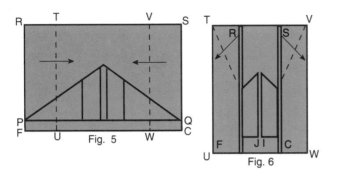

Fig. 5

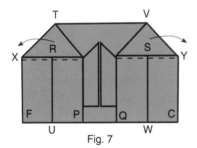

Fig. 6

Fig. 7

Fig. 8

5. Fold along TU and VW (Fig. 5) so that RF touches collar line J, and SC touches collar line I (Fig. 6).

6. Lift F, separating it from P, and open corner R so that point R falls on TU. Do the same with C and S (Figs. 6 and 7).

7. Fold back along XY (Figs. 7 and 8).

8. To make the sleeves, fold back only the back flap (Fig. 8).

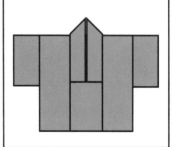

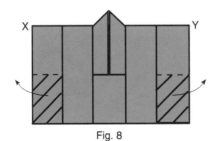

Lantern

1. Crease a square piece of paper as shown in Fig. 1 and then spread open.

2. Fold the four corners A, B, C, and D forward so that they meet at the center as in Figs. 2 and 3.

3. Turn over and fold the four corners E, F, G and H so that they meet at the center as in Fig. 4.

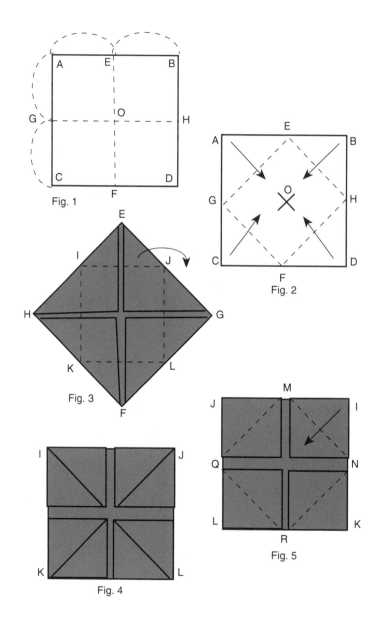

Fig. 1

Fig. 2

Fig. 3

Fig. 4

Fig. 5

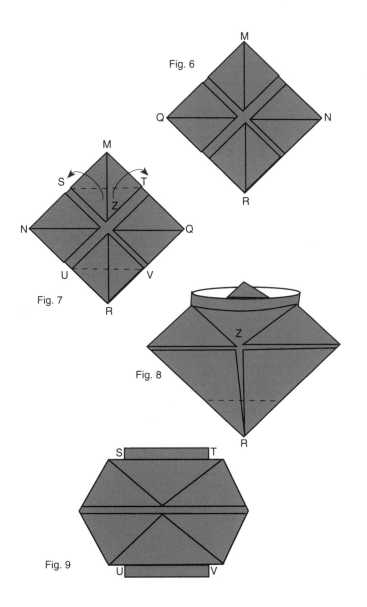

Fig. 6

Fig. 7

Fig. 8

Fig. 9

4. Turn the paper over once more and you will have Fig. 5.

5. Next, fold the corners I, J, K, and L forward once more to meet at the center. Turn the paper over and you will have Fig. 6.

6. Using both thumbs, push open MZ as in Figs. 7 and 8. Do the same with ZR and you will get Fig. 9.

Table

1. Fold a square piece of paper along GH and IJ (Fig. 1) so that edges AC and BD meet at center EF (Fig. 2).

2. Fold GI back along KL (Fig. 2) so that GI will be under HJ (Fig. 3).

3. Fold the top flap along MN (Fig. 3) so that HJ falls on KL (Fig. 4).

4. Make a crease along CM and DN (Fig. 4) and then pull out corners C and D (Fig. 5).

5. Turn the paper over and repeat steps 3 and 4.

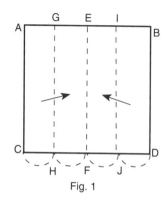
Fig. 1

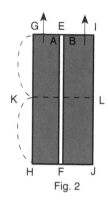
Fig. 2

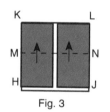
Fig. 3

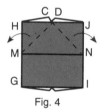
Fig. 4

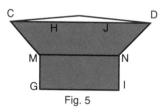
Fig. 5

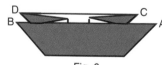
Fig. 6

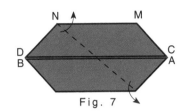

Fig. 7

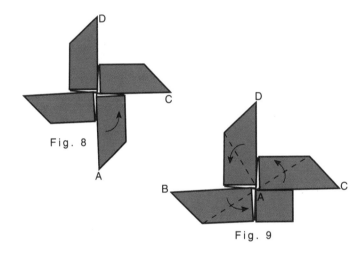

Fig. 8

Fig. 9

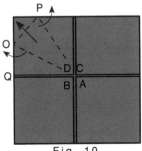

Fig. 10

6. Spread Fig. 6 out so that it looks like Fig. 7.

7. Fold D upward and A downward (Figs. 7 and 8).

8. Open corner A (Fig. 8) and bring point A to the center (Fig. 9).

9. Repeat step 8 at corners B, C, and D (Figs. 9 and 10).

10. Crease at OD and PD (Fig. 10) so that QD and JD meet at the center. Then crease at OP. Lift up D, folding along OP so that Q and J meet at the middle (Fig. 11) on DZ.

31

11. Repeat step 10 for the other corners A, B, and C (Figs. 11 and 12).

12. Fold along DR and DS (Fig. 12) so that DO meets DP at the center on DZ.

13. Repeat step 12 on corners A, B, and C (Fig. 13).

14. To make the legs stand, fold along TU (Fig. 13).

15. Repeat step 14 on corners C, A, and B (Fig. 14).

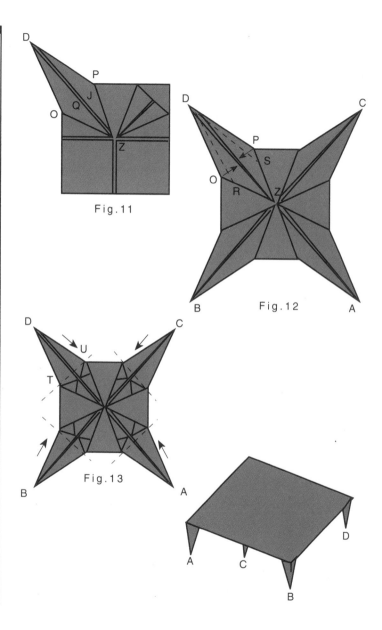

Fig.11

Fig.12

Fig.13

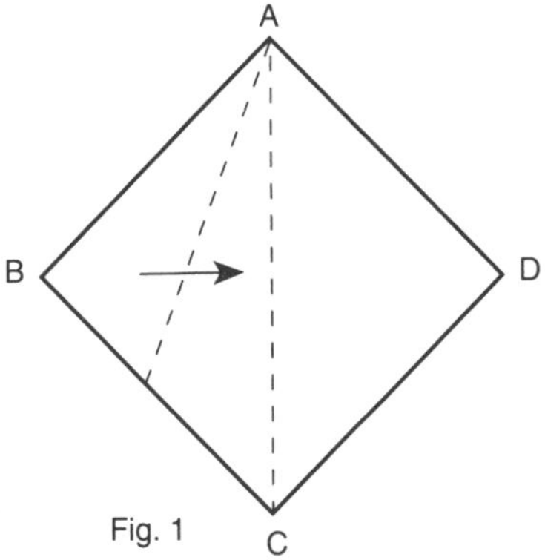

Fig. 1

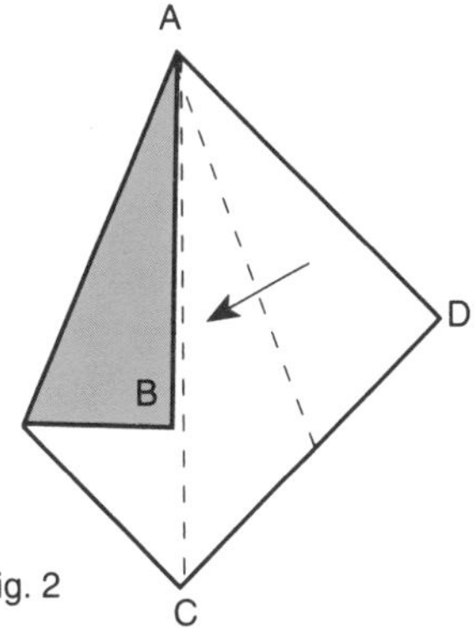

Fig. 2

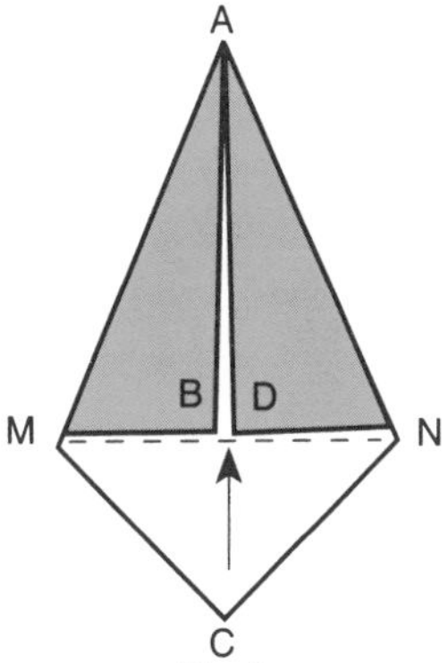

Fig. 3

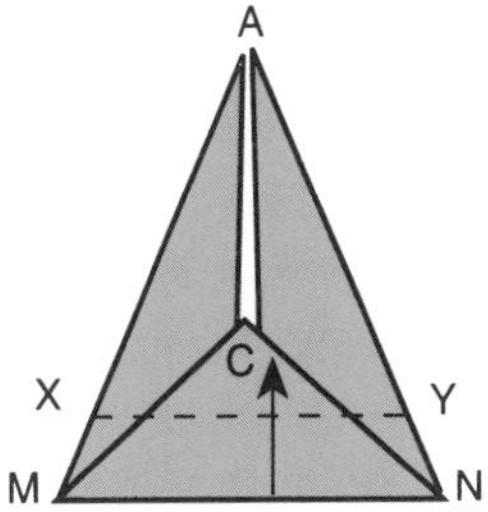

Fig. 4

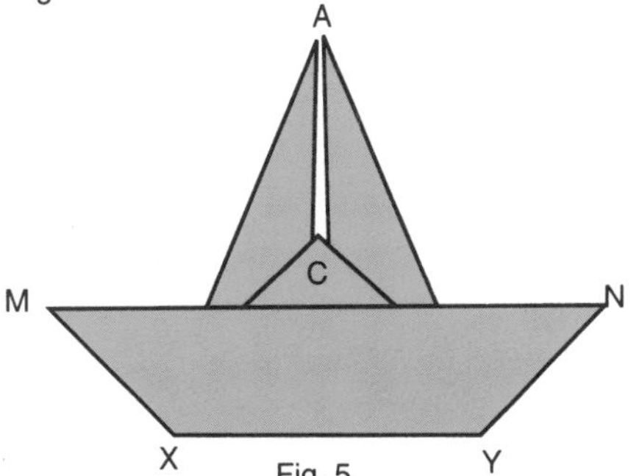

Fig. 5

Sailboat

1. Take a square piece of paper and fold it along line AC so that point B meets point D. Crease and then re-open as in Fig. 1.

2. Fold AB over to meet the center line AC (Fig. 2).

3. Do the same with AD so as to make Fig. 3.

4. Fold along line MN so that point C is above points B and D. See Fig.4.

5. To complete, fold along line XY so that points M and N look like Fig. 5.

Ship

1. Fold a square piece of paper down the center on line EF as shown in Fig. 1, crease, and then unfold.

2. Fold at GH and IJ so that edges AC and BD meet at the center line EF. This results in Fig. 2.

3. Fold at MN so that edge HJ reaches the center line XY, forming Fig. 3.

4. Pull out corners C and D in order to form Fig. 4.

5. Fold backwards at OP so that edge GI is directly under MN as shown in Fig. 5.

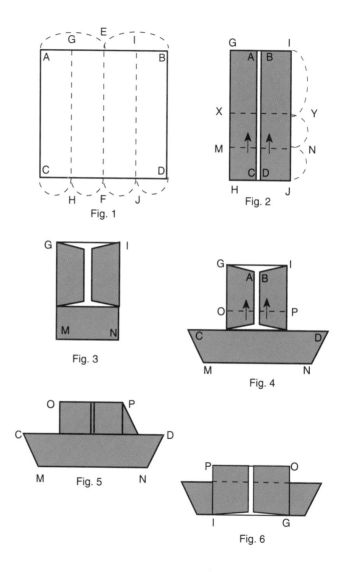

Fig. 1

Fig. 2

Fig. 3

Fig. 4

Fig. 5

Fig. 6

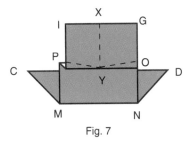

Fig. 7

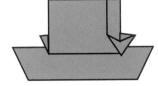

Fig. 8

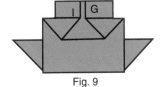

Fig. 9

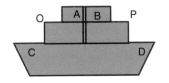

Fig. 10

6. Turn over to get Fig. 6.

7. Fold so that the edge IG is over and above PO as in Fig. 7.

8. Bring point G forward and to the left so that it is directly over X, which is in the center. Fig. 8 shows how this is done. Do the same with point I in order to get Fig. 9.

9. Turn over and you will have the ship shown in Fig. 10.

35

Wolf

1. Fold a square piece of paper along line BD (Fig. 1) so that corner C falls on corner A (Fig. 2).

2. Crease BE by bringing BC and BA down to fall on BD (Figs. 2 and 3).

3. Make another crease as in step 2 along FD. Then cut out two triangles at M and N (Fig. 4).

4. Now fold along BM and DN (Fig. 5) so that X falls on BC and Y falls on DC (Fig. 6).

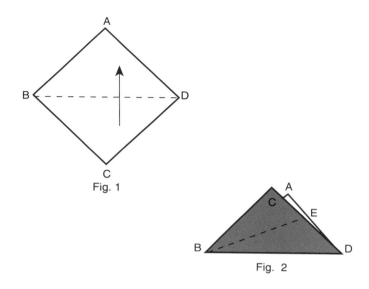

Fig. 1

Fig. 2

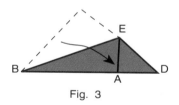

Fig. 3

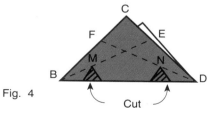

Fig. 4

Cut

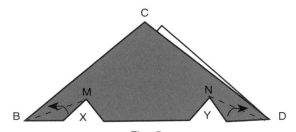

Fig. 5

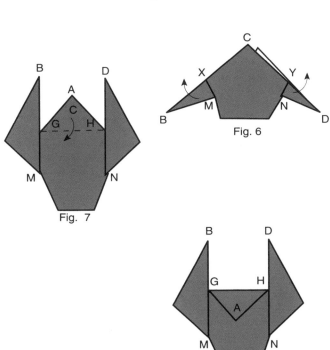

Fig. 7

Fig. 6

Fig. 8

Cut

5. Fold corners B and D upward (Fig. 6) so that BM and DN are almost vertical (Fig. 7).

6. Fold along GH (Fig. 7), bringing corners C and A forward (Fig.8).

7. Turn the paper over, draw the face, and cut out the mouth.

Bird

1. Fold a square piece of paper along AC (Fig. 1) so that corner B falls on corner D (Fig. 2).

2. Fold along EF (Fig. 2), bringing corners B and D to the left (Fig. 3). AE is a little less than one-half of the way down AD (Fig. 2).

3. Fold along GH (Fig. 3), bringing only corner D to the right while keeping B in place (Fig. 4).

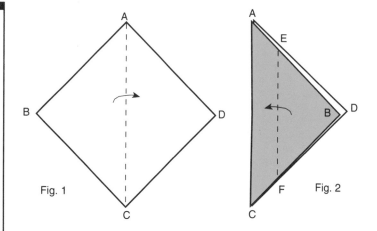

Fig. 1

Fig. 2

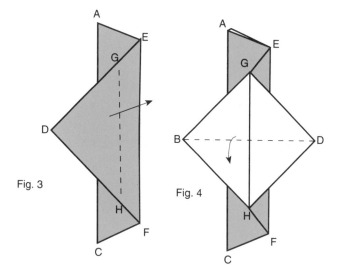

Fig. 3

Fig. 4

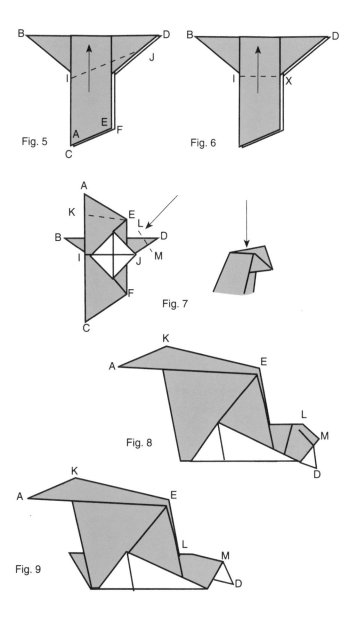

Fig. 5

Fig. 6

Fig. 7

Fig. 8

Fig. 9

4. Fold along BD (Fig. 4) so that edge AE falls on CF (Fig. 5).

5. Fold along IJ at a slant (Fig. 5) or horizontally along IX (Fig. 6) on the top flap of the body. Fold along KE, bringing A to the left (Figs. 7 and 8).

6. Repeat steps 5 and 6 on the other side.

7. To make the head, crease at LM (Fig. 7) and bring point D down between the flaps (Fig. 8).

Elephant

1. Fold a square piece of paper along lines AE and AF (Fig. 1) so that AB and AD meet at the center AC. See Fig. 2.

2. Fold along AC (Fig.2) so corner E falls on corner F. (Fig.3)

3 Fold along ON (Fig. 3) bringing point A forward and across to the right so that NA is about parallel to EC (Fig.4).

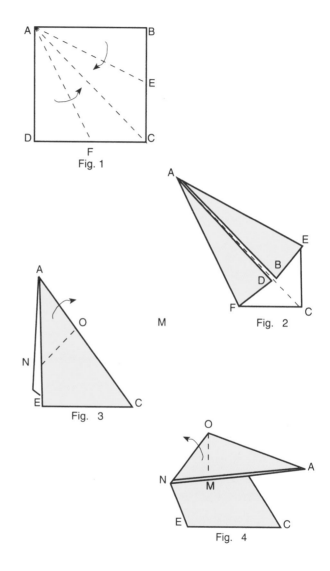

Fig. 1

Fig. 2

Fig. 3

Fig. 4

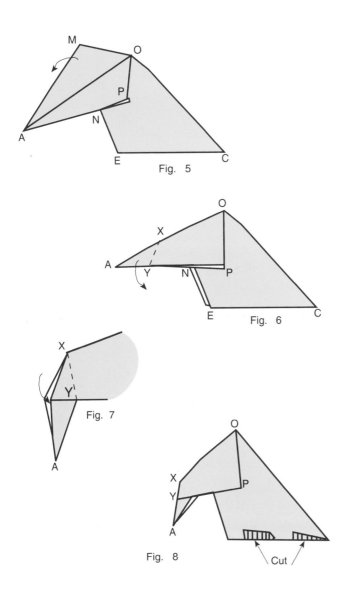

Fig. 5

Fig. 6

Fig. 7

Fig. 8

Cut

4. Lift the top flap at M (Fig.4) and open corner O, bringing point A across to the left so that OA falls almost on ON (Fig.5).

5. Fold point M back along OA (Figs. 5 & 6).

6. Crease XY (Fig. 6), separate the two flaps of the ears , and bring point A down between the flaps (Fig. 7).

7. Draw the eyes and cut out the legs and tail.

Fish

1. Fold a square piece of paper down the center at EF as shown in Fig. 1, crease, and then unfold.

2. Bring forward corners A and B until they meet along the center line EF, forming Fig. 2.

3. Fold at GH and IJ so that the edges KC and LD meet at the center line EF, as shown in Fig. 3.

4. Fold upward at MN so that HJ meets point E as in Fig. 4.

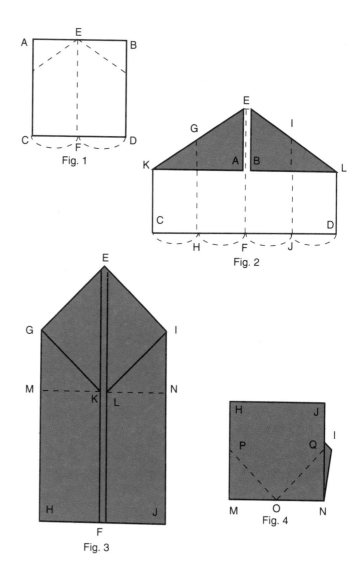

Fig. 1

Fig. 2

Fig. 3

Fig. 4

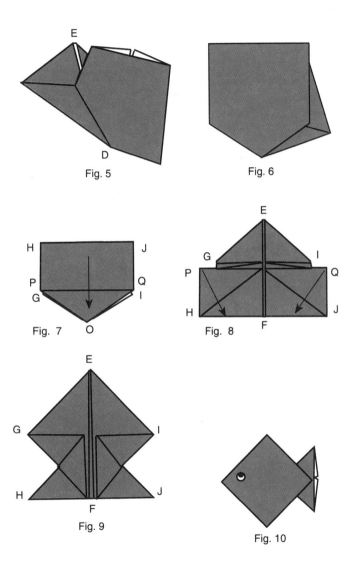

Fig. 5

Fig. 6

Fig. 7

Fig. 8

Fig. 9

Fig. 10

5. Pick up the paper and spread the two flaps HJ and GEI so that point M can be pushed up between them and extended as far as the center line EF. (Figs. 4, 5, and 6). Do the same with point N. The result is shown in Fig. 7.

6. Fold down the front flap at PQ in order to get Fig. 8.

7. Bend forward points P and Q so that they meet at F (Fig. 9).

8. Turn over and draw an eye as in Fig. 10.

Fox

1. Fold a square piece of paper along line EF (Fig. 1) so that AB falls on CD (Fig. 2).

2. Fold along IJ and KL (Fig. 2), so that edges AEC and BDF meet at center GH (Fig. 3).

3. Open corner F (Fig. 3) by lifting D toward the right while holding B in place resulting in (Fig. 4).

4. Repeat step 3 with ECA (Figs. 4 & 5) and turn the paper over (Fig. 6).

5. Fold along KM and IN (Fig. 6) so that edges OD and PC meet at the center (Fig. 7).

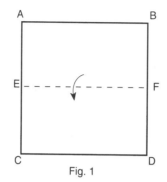

Fig. 1

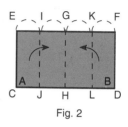

Fig. 2

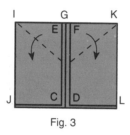

Fig. 3

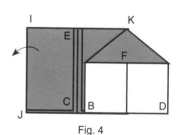

Fig. 4

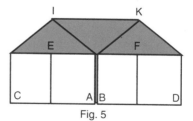

Fig. 5

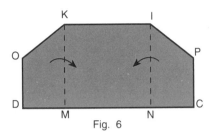

Fig. 6

6. Fold the top flap along EC (Fig. 7) so that N falls on P (Fig. 8).

7. Fold along EM (Figs. 8 & 9).

8. Fold the top flap along FE (Fig. 9) so that point M falls on K (Fig. 10).

9. Turn the paper over and repeat steps 6, 7, and 8 (Fig. 11).

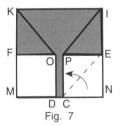

Fig. 7

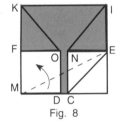

Fig. 8

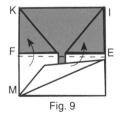

Fig. 9

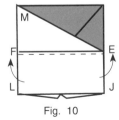

Fig. 10

10. Separate the two flaps by putting your thumb into I and your index finger into K from the back under EF (Fig. 11). Push back the middle part of the face with the other hand, and the ears, L and M, will stand up as shown in Fig. 12. Move your two fingers so that K and I meet.

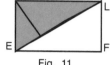

Fig. 11

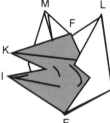

Fig. 12

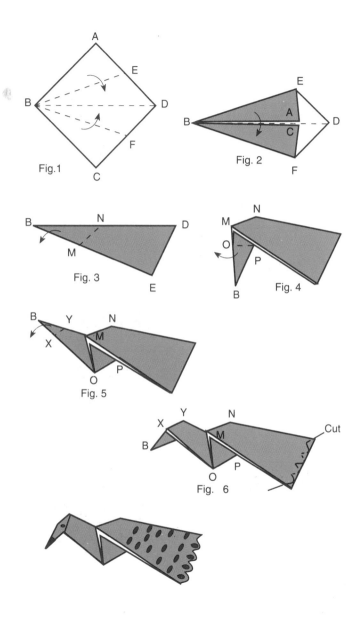

Fig.1

Fig. 2

Fig. 3

Fig. 4

Fig. 5

Fig. 6

Peacock

1. Fold a square piece of paper along lines BE and BF (Fig. 1) so that edges BA and BC meet at the center BD (Fig. 2).

2. Fold along BD (Fig. 2) so that E falls on F (Fig. 3).

3. Fold back point B along line MN (Figs. 3 & 4).

4. Fold along OP, bringing point B back and upward (Figs. 4 & 5).

5. Make the head by folding along XY, turning point B back and down-ward to theleft (Fig. 5).

6. Draw the feathers and cut their ends into curves (Fig. 6).

47

Frog

1. Fold a square piece of paper along line BC (Fig. 1) so that corner A falls on corner D (Fig.2).

2. Fold along EA (Fig. 2) so that point B falls on C (Fig. 3).

3. Open B (Fig. 3) and bring it over to the right, directly above D (Fig. 4). Place B on D and crease EF and EG.

4. Turn the paper over and repeat step 3 with C (Figs. 4 & 5).

5. Crease at XY and YC (Fig. 6) so that edges HC and IC meet along center line EC and open.

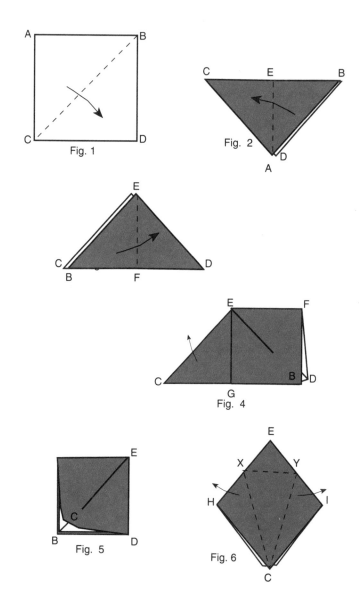

Fig. 1

Fig. 2

Fig. 4

Fig. 5

Fig. 6

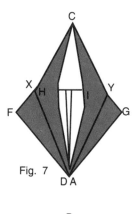

Fig. 7

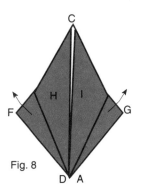

Fig. 8

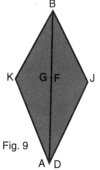

Fig. 9

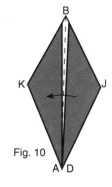

Fig. 10

Fig. 11

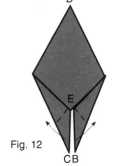

Fig. 12

6. Lift up C and fold at XY (Fig. 6) so that H and I meet at the middle on CD and CA, respectively (Figs. 7 & 8).

7. Turn the paper over and repeat steps 5 and 6 as shown in Fig. 9.

8. Fold the top flap to the left (Fig. 10) so that J now falls on top of K.

9. Turn over to repeat step 8 on the other side (Fig. 10) and then turn the figure upside down (Fig. 11).

10. To make the hind legs, lift B back between the flaps and to the right, and C to the left (Figs. 12 & 13).

11. Fold along LM and NO so that B and C are bent for ward again on both sides (Figs. 13 & 14).

12. Cut the top flap only, from D towards E about two-thirds of the way down the body flap (Fig. 13).

13. Fold along PQ and PR (Fig. 14) so that corners D1 and D2 stretch out on both sides of the body flap (Fig. 15).

14. Fold ST and UV (Fig. 15), making the two points D1 and D2 face upward towards A (Fig. 16).

15. Fold along WZ so that corner A comes down to the front (Fig. 16). Turn over (Fig. 17).

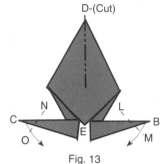

Fig. 13

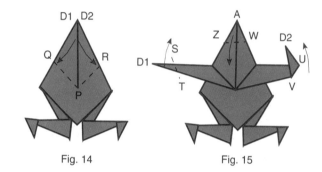

Fig. 14

Fig. 15

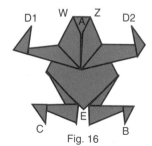

Fig. 16

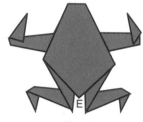

Fig. 17

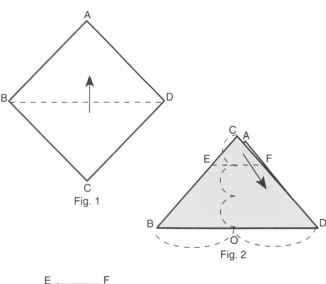

Fig. 1

Fig. 2

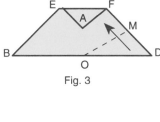

Fig. 3

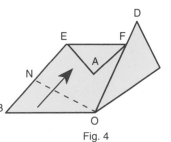

Fig. 4

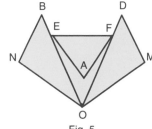

Fig. 5

Cat

1. Fold a square piece of paper along line BD (Fig. 1) so that corner C falls on corner A (Fig. 2).

2. Fold along EF (Fig. 2), bringing corners C and A forward (Fig. 3). EF is about one-third of the way down CO. (Fig. 2).

3. Fold along OM (Fig. 3), bringing corner D up so that OD meets F (Fig.4).

4. Repeat step 3 on the other side at ON (Figs. 4 & 5).

5. Turn the paper over and draw the face.

Giraffe

1. Fold a square piece of paper along lines AE and AF so that edges AB and AD meet at the center AC (Fig. 2).

2. Fold in half at AC (Fig. 2) so that AE falls on AF (Fig. 3).

3. Fold along OM and ON, inserting point M between the two body flaps. O is a little less than halfway down AE. (Figs. 3 & 4).

4. Fold in along AE (Fig. 5) so that point O is inside the body flap.

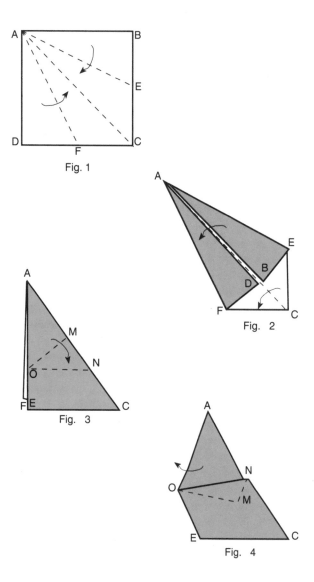

Fig. 1

Fig. 2

Fig. 3

Fig. 4

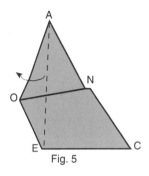

Fig. 5

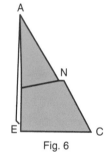

Fig. 6

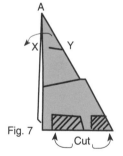

Fig. 7

Cut

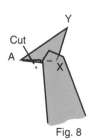

Fig. 8

5. Turn the paper over and repeat step 4 on the other side as in Fig. 6.

6. Cut out the legs (Fig. 7) and make slit XY on the back of the neck to make the neck and ears (Fig. 7 & 8). Cut off A (Fig. 8), and draw the eyes.

Penguin

1. Fold a square piece of paper along lines OP and MN (Fig. 1) so that edges AC and BD meet at center EF (Fig. 2).

2. Fold OM back along QR (Fig. 2) so that OM will be under PN (Fig. 3).

3. Fold along ST (Fig. 3) so that PN falls on QR (Fig. 4).

4. Make a crease along CS and DT (Fig. 4) and then pull out corners C and D (Fig. 5).

5. Turn the paper over and repeat steps 3 and 4 (Fig. 6).

6. Spread out Fig. 6. The result should look like Fig. 7.

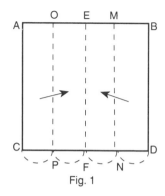

Fig. 1

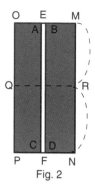

Fig. 2

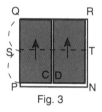

Fig. 3

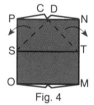

Fig. 4

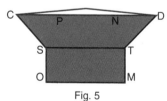

Fig. 5

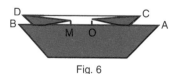

Fig. 6

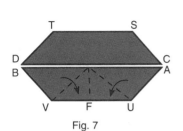

Fig. 7

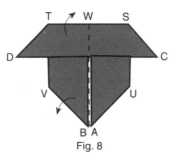

Fig. 8

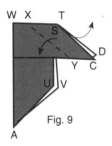

Fig. 9

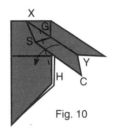

Fig. 10

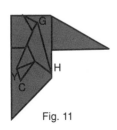

Fig. 11

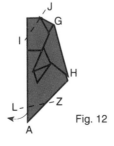

Fig. 12

7. Fold along FV and FU, bringing B and A downward to meet at the center (Figs. 7 & 8).

8. Fold in half along WA so that S and T, C and D, U and V meet respectively.

9. Fold along XY, bringing S and C in front (Figs. 9 & 10).

10. Fold again at GH, bringing YC forward (Fig. 11).

11. Do the same on the other side.

12. To make the head, fold along IJ and KJ (Fig. 13) pushing IJ back in between the body flaps (Fig. 14).

13. To make the feet, fold along LZ (Fig. 12) putting A in between the body flaps.

14. Do the same on the other side (Fig. 15).

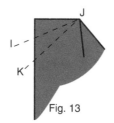

Fig. 13

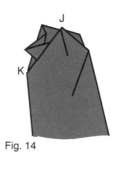

Fig. 14

Fig. 15

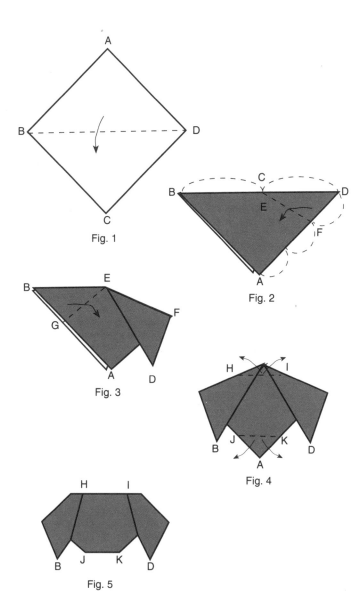

Fig. 1

Fig. 2

Fig. 3

Fig. 4

Fig. 5

Dog

1. Fold a square piece of paper along line BD (Fig. 1) so that corner A falls on corner C (Fig. 2).

2. Fold along EF (Fig. 2), bringing corner D forward (Fig. 3). Point F is about one-third of the way down DA. (Fig. 2.).

3. Repeat step 2 on the other side at EG (Figs. 3 & 4).

4. Fold back along HI and JK (Fig. 4), and then draw the face.

Pig

1. Fold a square piece of paper along line EF and IJ (Fig. 1) so that edges AB and CD meet at center GH (Fig. 2).

2. Fold in half along GH (Fig. 2) so that IJ falls on the back side of EF (Fig. 3).

3. Take the front flap and open corners E and F (Fig. 3) by bringing A to the right and B to the left so that they meet each other along HG. EK falls on MK and FL falls on NL (Fig. 4).

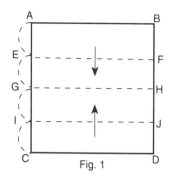

Fig. 1

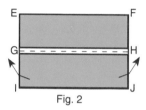

Fig. 2

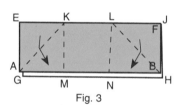

Fig. 3

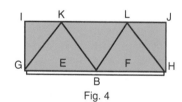

Fig. 4

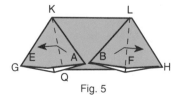

Fig. 5

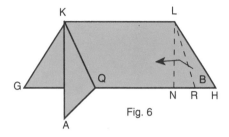

Fig. 6

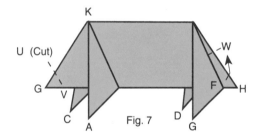

Fig. 7

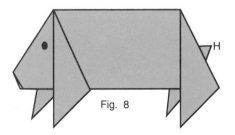

Fig. 8

4. Turn over and repeat step 3 with I and J (Fig. 5).

5. Fold along KQ (Fig. 5) so that KA falls on KE (Fig. 6).

6. Move B to the right (Fig. 5) so that edge LB falls on LH (Fig. 6).

7. Fold along LR (Fig. 6) so that LH falls on LN.

8. Turn over and repeat steps 5, 6, and 7 (Fig. 7).

9. Cut off point G at UV and draw dots for the eyes (Figs. 7 & 8).

10. To make the tail, fold along WF (Fig. 7) and push H in between the body flaps (Fig. 8).

Rabbit

1. Fold a square piece of paper along line EF (Fig. 1) so that corner A touches BD at the center (Fig. 2).

2. Fold forward along BD (Figs. 2 and 3).

3. Turn the paper over and fold along OG and OH (Fig. 4), bringing corners D and B forward to meet at C (Fig. 5).

4. Fold along XG and XH (Fig. 5), bringing corners D and B up and off O (Fig. 6). Point X then is not on GH but a little higher up on CO.

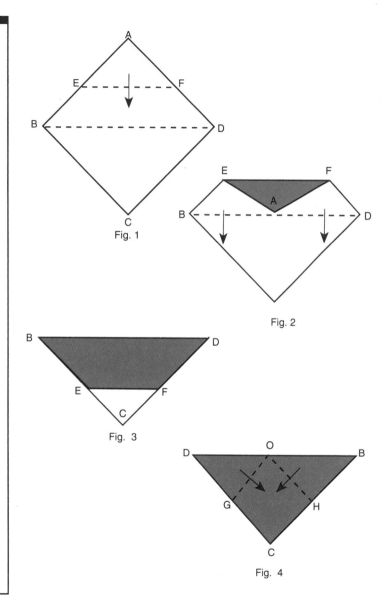

Fig. 1

Fig. 2

Fig. 3

Fig. 4

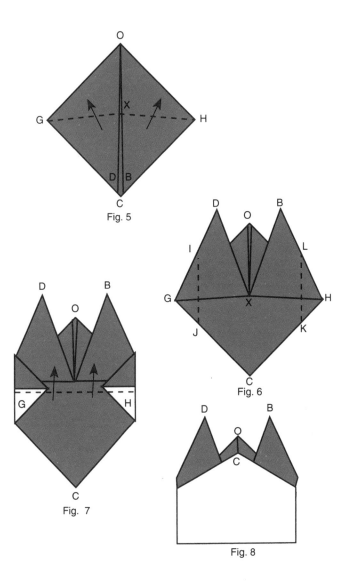

Fig. 5

Fig. 6

Fig. 7

Fig. 8

5. Fold along IJ and KL (Fig. 6) so that points G and H come forward on GH (Fig. 7).

6. Fold along GH (Fig. 7) so that corner C falls on O (Fig. 8).

7. Turn the paper over and draw the face and ears.

Swan

1. Crease a square piece of paper along line AD (Fig. 1) and then unfold.

2. Fold the edge AB forward to meet the center line AD. Do the same with the edge AC and the result will be Fig. 2.

3. Now fold the edge AE forward so that it reaches the center line AD and then repeat with edge AF. You now have Fig. 3.

4. Fold along the center line AD so that AG is on top of AH as in Fig. 4.

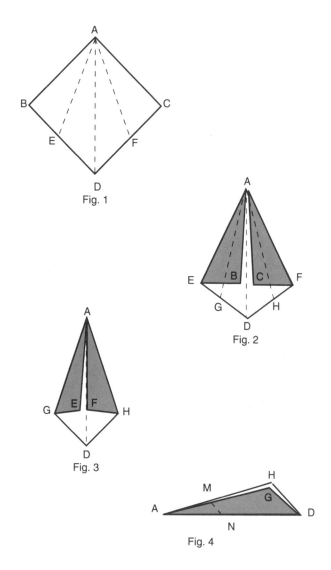

Fig. 1

Fig. 2

Fig. 3

Fig. 4

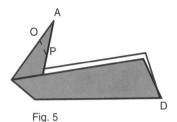

Fig. 5

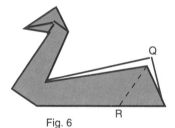

Fig. 6

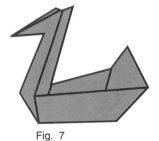

Fig. 7

5. To make the neck, pick up the paper with the open edge at the top and with corner A pointing to the left. Separate the two flaps slightly, bend back the pointed end at MN (Fig. 5), so that it is inserted between the body flaps. In doing so, the fold along the line AD in the neck portion will be reversed.

6. The head is formed in a similar way at OP. See Fig. 6.

7. The tail is formed at QR (Figs. 6 & 7) in the same manner as the neck and head.